Foreword

When I read the book "*My Glory*" I was awestruck by both the simplicity and the depth of the explanation provided. Personally, I have been in ministry 39 years, traveling around the world teaching and preaching the gospel of Jesus Christ. I am the overseer of Impact Apostolic Ministries for 18 years and I've read countless books on every aspect of ministry. To me, reading this book was like drinking a cold glass of water on a hot summer day! It is pure, unpretentious, and gives a true picture of the glory of God.

It took me back to one of my very early experiences with the Lord:

"One Saturday afternoon, a ministry colleague of mine and I were having a passionate conversation on a particular subject that we differed on greatly. The next day we were both at Sunday school and the very subject we differed on was being taught. I was delighted that the teacher pointed out every point I made to him. I relished in him being wrong and proudly volunteered to do the review. My plan was to reiterate the points I had made the previous day. As I stood there in front of the congregation, I had an open vision. The Lord rebuked me for wanting to lift myself up and cautioned me to *never steal his glory*. He told me that "every platform I have been given is provided for me to glorify him and to give him praise."

Prophetess Stennis's profound explanation of *his glory* and *his nature* shares with the reader a picture of *his majesty* and *his generosity*. The gentle explanation of how to invite him into our space and wait for him to accept our invitation gives the reader a true understanding of how we are in relationship with him because, he is God alone. Each chapter has golden nuggets of how to live in *his divine glory*, and *how to respect his glory*. We have the privilege to exhibit *his glory* by displaying our faith in Him. Quoting from this book "*His magnificent glory gives our lives the substance and value that we all desire*" and I know as Christians, we are all searching for our significance in him.

The first time I read the book, I was so moved I read it again! It was just as refreshing the second time around. From the beginning to the end, you will know that Nikhole spent time with the Lord to receive this needed information. As her apostle and friend, I am both excited and honored to write this foreword. I have watched Prophetess Nikhole Hatten-Stennis grow in grace and wisdom for the last 20 years.

As a wife and mother, I recently told her how much respect I have for her. She is a loving wife to retired Major JayCee Stennis Jr, raising three sons, works full-time, is a veteran of the United States Air Force, has her own jam company, and gives of herself to kinsmen and stranger alike without hesitation. Her eldest son just graduated from medical school, her middle son graduated with a master's degree in business, and her youngest is graduating from high school as team captain of the basketball team with a 4.0 GPA; noting that each of them have a relationship with Christ. She is one of the prophets on the presbyter of Impact Apostolic Ministries giving that same spirit of excellence exhibited to her peers. They look to her for counsel and support, both of which she freely gives including her time and energy. Her walk and her talk exude the Christ in her!! The book flows so seamlessly! Anyone who reads this book will be immensely blessed!!

Apostle K. Richardson

Table of Contents

Introduction

“MY GLORY”

For His Glory, We Will Do Anything

“Whether therefore ye eat, or drink, or whatsoever ye do, do all to the glory of God”.

1 Corinthians 10:31

Have you ever wondered what it truly means to know, manifest, or be a partaker of God's glory? When Christians gather for services, Bible studies, and conferences, you will often hear the expression "glory" and "glory to God". When we are on the receiving end of a bad situation, trouble that we are in, at the end of a storm in our lives we often think and express glory to God when these things cease to exist. When we get a diagnosis of some form of sickness or disease and when God sustains us, delivers us, or miraculously heals us, we often say "glory to God".

If we lose a loved one and are in mourning, our hearts are often heavy, and our minds need consoling to get through the grief process. It is the glory of God that lovingly repairs our hearts and in time allows our minds to remember the loss without feeling the pain of that loss. When we receive a desired marriage proposal, get married, receive a promotion, high honor, new idea, unexpected money, have the resources to pay our bills, spend time with people we love, have a baby, adopt a child, move into a new home, get a new car, pay off debt, pass exams, get accepted into institutions of higher learning, graduate, play sports of all kinds, get an invitation to play sports at the professional level, and the list could go on but ultimately, we understand that these things that are named all take place in this thing we call life.

In the process of living, we are admonished by God in 1 Corinthians 10:31 to “do all to the glory of God”.

So, while we are living our lives remember to receive into our souls what serves to refresh, strengthen, and nourish it unto eternal life. Each of us are figurative authors giving existence to an unwritten collective work (epistle) of the splendor that only belongs to God, hallelujah! (2 Corinthians 3:3).

This book will take you on an exploration of *every* aspect of Gods glory. Who His glory is meant to be with, what His glory is, when His glory is present with us, and how we should respond to His magnificent glory.

Chapter 1

Then and Now

"And if children, then heirs; heirs of God, and joint heirs with Christ; if so be that we suffer with him, that we may be also glorified together."

-Romans 8:17

Then: We were impure, and God is perfect. In the Old Testament, when the house of worship (temple/tabernacle) was completed, they placed the ark of the covenant in the Holy of Holies. After the priests sanctified themselves, atoned for their sins, and the people praised God, His glory filled the temple and the priests on the Day of Atonement could not perform their service because the glory of the Lord filled His temple (1 Kings 8:11 KJV).

The type of glory spoken of in 1 Kings 8:11 in the Hebrew is known as kabod. This word is found several times in the books of Genesis, Exodus, Deuteronomy, Ezekiel, Isaiah, Psalms, and Proverbs. Kabod appears as a magnificent manifestation of our creator. When it enters our world, we experience great joy, and our response is to reverence our God for being present with us.

God is spirit (John 4:24) and has no physical body which gives Him the ability to be constantly encountered (omnipresent).

Now: We are still impure, and God is forever perfect. Jesus became the atonement (propitiation) for our sins once for all forever. We now have the privilege of confessing our sins every day. Not once a year as in the Old Testament when people went to the temple to confess their sins once a year on the Day of Atonement. When we confess our sins (repent) God forgives us, wipes our slate clean, and removes our unrighteous deeds (1 John 1:9). God is pleased with us when we repent. Repentance is necessary to receive forgiveness for our sins. You may wonder why repentance is so important as it relates to our walk with God and how this directly affects how we honor Him and how we manifest His glory. Repentance is the *doorway* into the kingdom of God!

Jesus said in Matthew 3:2 to "repent for the kingdom of heaven is at hand." At hand means that the benefits of the kingdom are now within our reach! Some of those benefits of the kingdom are salvation, receiving the Holy Spirit, and to give Him glory.

Genuine repentance glorifies God! A repentant heart understands that the offense of sin before our holy God dishonors Jesus who died to redeem and deliver us from sin. A repentant heart acknowledges that God ALONE deserves all the honor and glory (Revelations 4:11).

As Christians/Disciples of Jesus Christ, we collectively are the temple of God. Teamwork and unity of the faith are our function because this is where God dwells. We were constructed for the purpose of worshipping Him. Because we are the temple of

God, it is through us that God reaches the world. Jesus is calling each of us because wherever we are as individual temples when we are walking in His ways, we make His presence and glory known to all nations. (1 Corinthians 6:19-20, 1 Corinthians 12).

Chapter 2

It's Not Yours

"Thine, O Lord, is the greatness and the Power and the glory, and the victory, and the majesty: for all that is in the heaven and in the earth is thine; thine is the kingdom, O Lord, and thou are exalted as head above all".

-1 Chronicles 29:11

Everything that exists belongs to God! He has the right to keep everything for Himself, but He is a loving and generous God who chooses to share all that He is and all that He has created with mankind. He does not need to pay or repay any of us, nor does He need to ask us for anything. The Lord spoke to me and said to tell His people that: "You don't command me to come into your space. You welcome me in, and I decide on whether or not I will accept your invitation".

This is a good time to share an example of why it is important to welcome Jesus into "our space(s)". Several years ago, while I was serving at a ministry in Texas, our congregation was invited to attend a revival at another church. This was the third night of the revival, and several leaders took the advice of another leader who spoke highly of the revival. She told us that God shows up each night mightily, and as leaders, we should all come to at least one night of the three-night revival. Then and now, I pray about all things before I say yes, so that I know that this is something that the Lord wants me to be a part of. I prayed and asked the Lord if I should go, and He gave me the go ahead to attend the revival on the third night. When we arrived at the church, I recognized a couple of vehicles with license plates that read "prophet", and upon entering the service, I saw multiple foot baths scattered in the center of the sanctuary. The pastor introduced the guest speaker for the night and took his seat. The church was filled to capacity with standing room only, so we stood in the very back of the church as the speaker introduced himself and then went into the message for the evening.

The speaker identified himself as a prophet and said that there were angels troubling the water in the foot baths. At this point of the service, the Spirit of the Lord spoke to me and said, "stay where you are, observe what you see, I am not in this".

I felt a peace from God and an alarm at the same time. The people in attendance didn't pay attention to the fact that the "prophet" didn't give any context to the word he spoke, no scripture was given which is the foundation for everything we do as servants of God, and he commanded God and the angels to heal and perform miracles that night. He even went as far as to say that the water in the foot baths was moving by the angels, but visibly, the water was completely still.

Everyone in the church that evening went at the command of the “prophet” to step into the foot baths. The music was high, and the people really wanted to see miracles and receive healing as a result of stepping into the foot baths.

All but two people put their feet in the foot baths. The “prophet” wasn’t pleased that everyone didn’t do as he commanded, and then began to speak curses over those who didn’t participate in his performance. Quietly, where I stood, I began to pray for the blood of Jesus to protect, guard, and cover us all.

The two people who did not participate were me and my armor bearer. To add insult to injury, the “prophet” told the people that to be blessed, they would need to give at least $100.00 dollars each but also said that there were people there who are required to give

$500.00- and $1000.00-dollar offerings.

This was and still is troubling because 2 Corinthians 9:7 tells us that each of us should give what we have decided in our heart to give, not reluctantly or under *compulsion,* for God loves a cheerful giver. Compulsion is the action or state of forcing or being forced to do something. Before you attend another service, pray, and prepare ahead of time so that you can "give what you have decided in your heart to give".

As we were leaving the church, our family decided to get something to eat. We went to a local restaurant and in walked the "prophet" from the revival. My husband recognized him and offered for him to sit with us, and he agreed. He began sharing with us where he was from, and some of the things that he has encountered in ministry. He said that God uses him to perform miracles and gave a specific detailed story that I still remember to this day. He has a perishner who is very wealthy and also very sick.

When the perishner calls him for prayer, he goes to see him and every time he lays hands on him to command a miracle and/or healing to come forth it happens, but only after he pays him a significant amount of money. This is a perpetual money exploitation and is not of God!

When God heals or performs a miracle, it is complete! It became evident to us that this servant was acting out of self interest and personal gain. As we were leaving the restaurant, we found out that after this speaker had raised all of the money in the offering, he had no ride back to his hotel. Our family offered to drive him to his hotel, and he accepted. We didn't agree with most of what the "prophet" said or did, but we recognize that even though our hearts were heavy because of the “prophets” ill gotten gain, we are still required to do our part and it is God who will judge (Matthew 12:36-37).

This is the example God wanted me to use, but unfortunately, I have witnessed this in varying degrees many times. It is fitting that if you are reading this and know that you have “commanded” God to come into your space, this would be a good time to repent and ask Him to forgive you.

Then pray this prayer: Jesus, I worship and praise you. You are great and greatly to be praised! The greatness, power, majesty, and glory all belong to you. I honor you, for you are head over all things and judge of each of us. Thank you for everything you have done in redeeming me and bringing me into your kingdom. I pray that I will never become so familiar that I think it is appropriate for me to command you to do anything on my behalf. I pray that when I welcome you into my space, that you will accept the invitation. In Jesus name I pray, AMEN.

Chapter 3

It Belongs to Me

"I am the Lord: that is my name: and my glory will I not give to another, neither my praise to graven images".

-Isaiah 42:8

The Lord spoke to me and said "Tell my people that MY GLORY belongs to me and me alone. I have not and I will not give it to another, neither my praise to graven images".

The glory in Isaiah 42:8 in the Hebrew language is known as the kabod glory of God. This glory is the weighty masculine glory of God. The kabod glory demands that we give reverence, honor, and respect to the manifestation of His presence.

In Hebrew, the word kavad functions as both "glory" and "liver". There is a direct connection between the fruit of what is said and what is done. We must look inside ourselves and understand that the whole cellular structure of creation is written within us. The things we do on the outside are based on what is going on in the inside. When the Bible was written in Hebrew, people understood that the Hebrew language through concepts of body (biology), and the use of the word in seed form is directly correlated to agriculture.

So, let's look at the heaviest internal organ which is the liver to see what it is showing us about God's glory. The weightiness of the liver tells us that the glory of God has to do with being a heavy substance. In 2 Corinthians 4:17, Paul connects the weightiness of God's glory when comparing light momentary afflictions with an eternal “weight” of glory.

In terms of size, the liver is the greatest compared to all other internal organs, just as great is the glory of the Lord (Psalm 138:5). Our liver is important to a host of other body functions. Some examples of what the liver does are: it regulates sugar, protein, fat, and filters out toxins. It also stores nutrients and distributes blood through the hepatic artery. When we glorify God knowing that He is vital to every function of our lives, we rightly process the weight of the glory that is due to His name.

How much weight (glory) are we giving Him in our lives? How much weight (glory) does His word carry in our thoughts and in our deeds? Does His word filter out our sins (toxins), and rid us of them like the liver filters out toxins in our natural body and rids us of waste? The glory of God covers us on the outside and fulfills us on the inside. Both connect us to Jesus the door, and the only true way to experience the weighty glory of God.

In the past, I found myself repenting for lifting up and displacing where God's glory is supposed to be given which is *solely* to Him. In the past, I have followed leaders in the church in the wrong manner. Whether it was in my local church, at church conferences, or watching a televangelist, when leaders spoke with power, authority, and might, I did not see them as a vessel used by God, but unknowingly, I found myself displacing God's glory by magnifying the person when I clearly needed to magnify God and thank Him for His leaders.

This warrants an explanation, so "you shall know the truth, and the truth shall make you free" (John 8:32). I pray that this explanation will "make you free". I thought that I was following the scripture that states “follow me as I follow Christ (1 Corinthians 11:1) as it pertains to how I followed leadership in the church and unfortunately, I have been under several leaders that attempt to use God to profit themselves. Early on in ministry, I didn’t recognize that I was open and susceptible to misguided leadership. Our very nature can invite sinful habits and self-righteous attitudes. Leaders are human beings with the same propensity to sin, the difference is we are held to a higher standard in God, and by the people that we serve. If not handled properly, being a leader in the church can be a dangerous position to be in, and if a leader is puffed up or rogue in nature, this will grieve the Holy Spirit.

God appoints leaders to spiritually shepherd His people, not to build a successful organization or programs for their own gain. We have more than enough organizations and programs in the world. As leaders, I hope that we will return our efforts to building up His people and His kingdom. There are thousands of leaders in the body of Christ who have so much, but they give very little. If you are a leader in the church reading this book, God says to "open up your bowels of compassion and give" (1 John 3:17). There are many of our brothers and sisters who are suffering and if you have plenty, please give. Prayer is the foundation/beginning and at the end of prayer, God is calling for us to give.

Are we stealing God's glory? It would be wise for us to examine ourselves, our thoughts, and our motives. God takes His glory very seriously! It is blasphemous when we take any part of His glory for ourselves and when we purport His glory onto others. When we are selfish, insecure, and proud, these character flaws are open doors to stealing God's glory.

This happens through what we say and what we do. Worldly influences that cause us to dye our hair strange colors is just one example of our desire to be seen. If we wear inappropriate clothing that is to tight, too short, etc., this is with a desire to be seen. This behavior is expected of those who don't profess the name of Jesus Christ, but when we say that we are a Christian, these undesirable actions weaken the body and bring dishonor to His name (Isaiah 48:11 KJV). When we dress in a manner that tempts others, we purpose ourselves to lead others astray. When we open our mouth to use profane language, as a Christian, we pollute His name! The list goes on, and I am sure that you can see the picture that is being painted. We should all examine ourselves and repent of the things that are not like

Him. Whether we eat or drink, or whatever we do, do all to the glory of God (1 Corinthians 10:31).

Now, let's look at the second part of Isaiah 42:8 which reads "neither my praise to graven images". I have traveled the world, and for as long as I can remember, I have been fascinated with unicorns. Over the years, I collected and was given unicorns as gifts. I even (before knowing any better) had a unicorn tattooed on my leg when I was in the military. Many years ago, while in prayer, God told me that my fascination with unicorns had become an idol. I was very young in my walk with the Lord, so I thought surely, I heard wrong as my fascination was harmless. When I would pray and then listen for God's voice/instruction, for a while, I would always hear from Him that my desire for my unicorn collection was idolatrous.

I had a curio cabinet that displayed my unicorns in my home, and one day, I decided to put all of the unicorns I had in a large box to give them away because some of them were quite expensive (Lladro, Swarovski, etc.) I drove around with those unicorns in the trunk of my car for several weeks. It was so bad that I couldn't even use my trunk when I went grocery shopping because the box of unicorns was taking up all the space in my trunk.

Finally, I removed the large box and placed all the unicorns in a heavy weight black trash bag. I took the large black trash bag out on my back patio and told God that He means more to me than anything. That day, I destroyed my unicorn collection, but I gained a greater understanding of what it really means to obey God, and to be free to praise Him. I don't know what images or idols you have set up in your life, but I can tell you that it is important for each of us to get rid of them out of obedience to God. The dictionary definition of an idol can be anything that we revere, give devotion too, or that is used as an object of worship. Essentially, idols (graven images) are false gods that can't see, hear, or help us and they have no feet or hands according to Psalm 115:4-8. When we make them, we become like them, and I don't believe that any of us want to be mute, blind, deaf, and missing limbs.

Each choice we make that doesn't put God first in our lives opens us up to worshipping idols. The best way we can not fall prey to idols is to spend time with God, read His word daily, and pray often.

God will not give His glory to another because ALL glory, honor, and praise belong to Him alone. He will not allow

His works to be stolen and credit given to false gods or people who take credit for what he does. It is theft and immoral for us to take credit for what we have not done. It is God alone who created the heavens and the earth. Everything was created for Him, by Him, and through Him. We are partakers of all that he has created. He made us and that alone should be enough to make us want to give Him glory for all that he

has done, is doing, and will do
in our lives.

Chapter 4

How to Obtain It

"But we all with open face beholding as in a glass the glory of the Lord, are changed into the same image from glory to glory, even as by the Spirit of the Lord".

-2 Corinthians 3:18

The Greek word for glory in this scripture is "doxa". Doxa is a feminine noun that describes the nature of the glory of God in His magnificence, commanding respect, and excellence. The part of this scripture that is magnified for me is "beholding as in a glass the glory of the

Lord". This means that we are looking into a mirror. When you stand in front of a mirror and look into it, what do you see?

Naturally, we see our own reflection. But God is saying that what we see in the mirror when we are in Him is "His glory". You see, glory to glory is not going from one state of euphoria to another. It is not going from one state of being lost and then being found by God. To go from glory to glory, is to be ever changing into the likeness of Jesus Christ and to increase in glory continually being changed into what we were created to be. It is to be conformed into the image and likeness of God.

When we give our lives to Jesus, we are sealed until the day of redemption. The Holy Spirit from the day of Salvation is in us. When we receive the baptism by fire (Matthew 3:11), this consuming fire convicts us, seals us, teaches us, reminds us, comforts us, empowers us, equips us, bears fruit through us, and guides us into all truth. The Holy Spirit is our constant helper to remind us of who we are in Jesus Christ and equipping us daily for His kingdom come, His will be done, on earth as it is in heaven.

It is in the image and likeness of God that He created us (Genesis 1:26-28). This is not to say that we live perfect lives in this mortal state, but it is vital in our everyday living to remember the one who saves, the one who loves, the one who feels our pain, disappointment, and cares for us every single day of our human existence.

Jesus sits with us by His Spirit when we are in places of indecision, and if we ask Him for help, He will come in and help us. We may not receive the answer that we want, but He will give us what we need. As He helps us, we are being changed into His image. If we resist Him because we don't like the answer that He gives in places of indecision, we take on attributes that are not healthy and go at it in our own strength. This becomes so tiring, that we start to believe that God doesn't care for us. This is far from the truth; you see He loves us so much that He will allow us to choose the pace of how we are transformed into His image. If you look at your life, what are the things that you value the most? What does your daily routine look like? How much time do you spend praying? How much time do you spend reading the Bible? How much time do you spend helping someone else besides yourself?

After you take the time to contemplate and answer these questions, go look in the mirror. Yes, I said to go look into an actual mirror and don't look away, don't look into the mirror quickly, but take a couple of minutes and really look at your face without anyone in that room but you. Now, say this scripture out loud: “But we all with open face beholding as in a glass the glory of the Lord, are changed into the same image from glory to glory, even as by the Spirit of the Lord” (2 Corinthians 3:18).

I used this same scripture in the beginning of this chapter to emphasize the significance of repeating the importance of its meaning. When we repetitively read, speak, teach, and live out the words of the Bible, we create long-term memory by eliciting or enacting strong chemical interactions at the synapse of our neurons which is where neurons connect to other neurons in the brain. This is important because, repetition creates the strongest learning. For example, when we were children, we were implicitly taught how to tie our shoes. As we get older, tying our shoes becomes wrote in memorization. We don't think about it, we just do it. When we attend elementary school, we explicitly learn multiplication which relies on repetition. Then when we get to learn other forms of math like algebra, calculous, and equations, we realize that multiplication is a main tool in skillfully tackling the more complex mathematical subjects.

These examples bring me back to how do we obtain God's glory. When we go to church, talk about God with friends and family, and read the Bible, we are implicitly learning complex information without the awareness of what has been learned. We gain the knowledge of God and His word through the absence of consciously accessing knowledge.

Our brains take the absence of consciously accessible

knowledge like the belief that our parents love us, and the belief that there is a God, and then involves our working memory and attention to explicitly give significance to what we learn and hold dear.

If you are a disciple/follower of Christ/Christian, its never too late to stop living out the concept of "garbage in, garbage out (GIGO)". This term is used by many, but the concept is that poor quality of output is determined by the quality of input. If your greatest desire is to please God and to partake in His glory when you look at yourself in the mirror, evaluate your daily life to see how much of your life looks like God, and how much of your life looks like the world.

If your desire is to please Him, the acronym GIGO will change in your life to "God in, God out (GIGO)" when you decide that you desire that the reflection in the mirror is to look more like God through what you say and how you treat people, than what you once looked like when you tried to adapt to the things of this world.

Now look in the mirror by yourself once more and say out loud “God in, God out”, Jesus I seek to please you! I want to be where you are. I want to walk like you and talk like you. Please work on me Lord as I continue to be changed into your image and likeness.

Chapter 5

Presence

"And the Word was made flesh and dwelt among us (and we beheld his glory, the glory as of the only begotten of the Father) full of grace and truth."

-John 1:14 KJV

Now, let's lay the groundwork, and discuss a familiar word mentioned in the assembly/church, but not found by name in the Bible. In the Hebrew, it is Sh'cheenah, but we say Shekinah glory, which means to dwell on earth, divine visitation, and presence.

We are going to expound on each to give understanding of God's Shekinah glory. The Shekinah glory of God walked among us when Moses told the Israelites that God was in the midst of the camp to deliver them and give their enemies over to them in Deuteronomy 23:14.

God visited Elijah when he stood at the opening of the cave waiting for God to approach in 1 Kings 19: 11-13. First came the strong wind, then the earthquake, the fire, and then the Lord came in the form of a quiet voice. God visited Elijah again when he challenged four hundred prophets of Baal in 1 Kings 1: 20-40.

In 2 Chronicles 7:1 King Solomon dedicated the first temple and when he finished praying fire came down from heaven and consumed the burnt offering and the sacrifices and the glory of the Lord filled the temple.

Aaron, Nadab, Abihu, and seventy elders including Joshua went up Mount Sinai because God told them to, and they all met God's presence and were consumed by His holiness. God then commanded Moses to go farther up the mountain and a cloud covered the mountain. The glory of the Lord rested on Mount Sinai and the cloud covered it for six days (Exodus 24:19).

The Shekinah glory mainly seen as either a cloud or fire was a visible manifestation of His glory. God also manifests His glory by light that we cannot look at without experiencing immediate death.

God's glory and His presence are one. No sin is permitted in His presence. (Exodus 33:18-23).

The Prophet Isaiah prophesied the birth of Jesus thirty times over 700 years before the Lord was born. (Matthew 1:23; Isaiah 7:14). Jesus coming as Immanuel "God with us", is the total embodiment and evidence of God's Shekinah glory.

The Jewish encyclopedia describes Shekinah as the "created splendor of light which sometimes takes on human form". The birth of Jesus as God in the second person of our Triune god embodied flesh and came to dwell (Shekinah) among us. (John 1:14).

What was once invisible became visible because Jesus was fully God and fully man at the same time (Colossians 2:9). God is not just glorious; He is glory itself! When Jesus transfigured before Peter, James, and John, He revealed

His glory to man. (Matthew 17: 1-2).

Many years ago, while living in Texas, I decided to put God in His rightful place in my life which is first above all. With the concurrence /approval of my spouse for the three years that we lived in Texas; I was a stay-at-home mom. I was determined to get to know God. I gave my life to Him twice. Once at the age of nine, and then again at the age of twenty-two. Yes, I know that once in salvation is all that is required, but because I wasn't versed on what is stated in the scriptures, at the age of twenty-two, I gave my life to Him again to be certain that I belonged to Him.

Honestly, I'm glad for Jesus' saving grace, but I am overjoyed that my redeemer lives! During my time in Texas, I read the Bible cover to cover three times. I prayed, fasted, and as the Spirit of the Lord lead me, I read books by Christian authors, and sought

God's face every day. When I faced sickness, obstacles, trials, trouble, and tribulations, I found comfort in knowing that God's presence was always there with me.

One day as I was driving to pick up our son from Christian school, I parked my car, and it began to drizzle outside. When I got out of my car, I didn't see a need to grab an umbrella for such light rain, so I proceeded to walk to the school's main entrance. As I walked down the sidewalk, I looked up, and the rain that was falling looked like little flecks of light. Then I heard the Lord say, “My glory falls on you like rain”.

Immediately, I began to weep and thanked God for allowing me to experience His presence in such a tangible beautiful way. Jesus is the light of the world. He is the perfect expression of Shekinah glory. God is the same yesterday, today, and forever. He made His presence known in both the

Old and New Testament, and He is still making His presence known today.

He came as the lamb, and His second coming will be as the lion is sooner than we think. In Jesus second coming, He will dwell with us forever and His Shekinah glory will be as the sun forevermore (Revelations 1:16-18).

All these examples were provided to encourage you to get into His presence. In His presence there is fullness of joy

and everything that you need
can be found in His presence.

Chapter 6

I Am Always With You

"When Christ, who is our life, shall appear, then shall ye also appear with him in glory".

-Colossians 3:4

Before we can say “when Christ, who is our life, shall appear, then shall ye also appear with Him in glory”, we must first be assured that we are in Christ.

I cannot write this without the thought that there will be some who will read this book, that have not had the conversion experience.

Over the years serving in leadership in several churches, it has become painstakingly clear that there are many who come to church for years and think that as long as they come to church, they are saved. I have had people who have joined churches and become members of local churches who have never received the conversion experience. When asked why some simply say it is because they were never asked to give their lives to Christ, and they assumed that becoming a member of the church brought them to salvation.

The conversion experience is being saved from sin through Salvation that only comes by giving our lives to Jesus Christ! Because Salvation in Jesus saves us from sin, having an understanding of what sin is will help us to know why we say the "sinner's prayer" and why we who are already saved need to continue to repent of the sins (offenses) we commit against God's word.

Sins are transgressions against divine law. Sin can occur in the thoughts we think, words we speak, and in immoral, selfish, shameful, harmful actions that we commit. Sin is the glory of God not honored. The wonderful thing about God is he doesn't keep a record of our sins if we confess our sins, he is faithful and just to forgive our sins, and to cleanse us from all unrighteousness (1John1:9).

When Jesus says for us to "repent" and be converted" (Acts 3:19), He is telling us to change our minds. We change our minds by feeling and showing remorse for doing the wrong thing. Now that repentance has taken root in our hearts, we can be converted so that we have a place forever with Him in the kingdom of heaven (Matthew 18:3).

With the understanding that because of the fall of Adam in the Garden of Eden, we are all born into sin, if you have never given your life to Christ, but you desire to be a citizen of the kingdom of heaven, this is where I will lead you through the prayer of salvation. It doesn't matter what you have done in the past, what matters is what you are going to do right now.

Say this prayer with me "Dear Lord Jesus, I know that I am a sinner, and I confess my sins and ask for your forgiveness. I repent of my sins. I turn from my sins and invite you to come into my heart. Be the Lord of my life. I trust and follow you as my Lord and Savior forever".

If you prayed this simple prayer with me, you are now a born-again believer/follower of Jesus Christ. Welcome to the family of God! Going forward, spend time with God daily by praying and reading the Bible. If you don't have a church home, visit a couple of churches, and pray about the church you are considering joining. Most importantly, ensure that the church you join has a strong biblical foundation.

You will know this by whether they are giving guidance and instruction based on the Bible or their own philosophies. Always choose a church based on biblical principles/instruction. Because it is the word of God that will correct, inspire, and ultimately give you a firm foundation. God has a plan for each of our lives. It is up to us to walk in

His ways so we can fulfill our purpose.

At Salvation, we become the spiritual seed of Christ. We figuratively die with Him on the cross, are buried with Him, and are raised with Him into newness of life at His resurrection. Now, we are seated with Him in heavenly places. As a part of the new creation in Christ we are imputed with His righteousness.

The "old" you is dead because you have been born from above into spiritual union with Christ. Your "new" life is hidden with Jesus in God. It is Him that you now live and move and have your being in. Being born again means that we are dead to sin, and that the power of sin has been broken in our lives! The day is coming when our bodies will be made perfect as we will be with Jesus and see Him as He really is. On that day, all that are in Christ will be changed in a moment, in the twinkling of an eye, at the last trump.

The dead in Christ shall rise first, and then those who are still alive and remain on earth shall be caught up together with all the believers into the clouds to meet the Lord in the air. We shall be with Him forever! My God, on that wonderful day, Jesus Christ who is our life, will be revealed, and then we also will be revealed with Him in glory.

Prayer:

"Thank you, Jesus, for the blessed hope that is before us that trust in you as Lord and Savior. Thank you that I and my brothers and sisters in Christ are in you and you are in us. The day is coming when you will return to take us home to be with you in heaven.

Help us to set our minds on the things that are above, kingdom purpose, and not the things of this world. We desire to live our lives in a way that is pleasing in your sight. In Jesus' name, AMEN.

Chapter 7

Eternity/Eternal

"Now unto God and our Father be glory forever and ever"

-Philippians 4:20

"But may the God of all grace, who called us to His eternal glory by Christ Jesus, after you have suffered a while, perfect, establish, strengthen, and settle you."

-1 Peter 5:10

God is both Lord and Father to all believers. The ultimate purpose of our lives is centered on glorifying God alone. God is the beginning, and the end of creation, not man (Revelations 1:8). No matter what we are faced with, there is always an opportunity for us to glorify God, reflect on His greatness, and He can change our temporal situations into eternal purpose. There is no adversity without an opportunity to glorify God. Every blessing of our lives are opportunities to magnify the greatness of God.

Glory is due to God and our Father throughout every age until God is no more. The hosts of heaven who did not fall and by mankind who have been or will be recovered glory is justly due and will be given to Him alone.

We were created to experience and reflect God's glory that comes from beyond this world. His sovereignty and lasting majesty can only come down from above.

Time after time, God continues to give us grace that we did not earn but that He gives because of His great love for us. Everything that saves our souls from the end time and brings us into the eternal God is the expression "the God of all grace".

As humans, we bear the image of God. As image bearers, we have free will and delegated authority to make our own decisions. This makes us accountable for our own choices. We belong to God because He called us to His eternal glory in Christ Jesus. We learn the word grace before we understand the meaning of it. It is when we need grace that we begin to feel what it truly means. We need “all grace” to heal our wounded souls. We need “the God of all grace” because He is the fountain of living water, ever flowing in compassion for His people.

No one enjoys or likes to suffer, but suffering in God is meant to produce strength, restoration, and steadfastness. God sustains us in our suffering and will not let us be overcome by it. We are being renewed and we will be raised from the dead to live together forever with our Lord and Savior Jesus Christ.

So, *don't* lose heart! Our suffering and afflictions are

temporary. These afflictions are producing an eternal weight of glory beyond anything that we could imagine or compare it to in this life (2 Corinthians 4:17).

We cannot bypass suffering if we desire to reign with Him (2 Timothy 2:12). As believers, our eternal destiny is to be restored, and established, with a firm foundation that will by the grace of God allow believers to share in the glory of Jesus Christ forever.

Remember, we all have the power to choose. When the Lord is revealed from heaven, He will deal out eternal punishment to unbelievers, but share His eternal glory with His saints (2 Thessalonians 1: 6-10).

When Jesus returns will you be an unbeliever awaiting the sentence of eternal destruction? Or are you comforted in knowing that though you have to suffer for a little while, eternal glory is waiting for you?

The glory of God is intrinsically valuable and needed for cvery function of our purpose driven meaningful lives! His eternal glory is manifested in us by our faith in Him. Glory is substantiated through our ability to persevere through the tests and trials that we face. His magnificent glory gives our lives the substance and value that we all desire.

Eternally in His Service,

Prophetess Nikhole Hatten-Stennis

Glossary Strong's-Lite Concordance

1. Doxa – Etymology-Greek: glory "is one of the most common praise words in scripture.
2. Kavod /Kavad– (n.m.) (K-V-D) Etymology-Hebrew: glory, importance, weight, heaviness
3. Kabod – (n.m.) (K-B-D) Etymology-Hebrew:

glory, important, honor, majesty, to be heavy

4. Shekinah –(sekinah)- Etymology – Hebrew: glory, settling of the divine presence of God
5. Ki bed (v.)-Etymology – Hebrew: respect or honor
6. Tipharah (n.f.) – Etymology- Hebrew: of rank, renown, as attributed of God.

(922, 1391, 1411, 2570, 3513, 4149, 4766, 5092, 6286, 8597)

Footnotes

- www.jewishencyclopedia.com(shekinah)
- Wikipedia
- Websters Dictionary

MY GLORY

Reflections

- How does the reading relate to your life?
- Before you read this book, what was your perception of God's glory?

- How will you apply what you read to your present life?
- How will you connect what you learned about God's glory going forward?

Made in the USA
Columbia, SC
13 June 2024

36552432R00074